The Pip Zips!

By Carmel Reilly

Vim gets a big pip.

She zips to the ant hub.

Vig hits the pip.

The pip zigs and zags!

The pip zips into a gap.

Vig pops wax on a pin.

Vig fits the pin into the gap.

The wax gets the pip.

Vig hits the pip.

CHECKING FOR MEANING

1. What happened when Vig hit the pip the first time? *(Literal)*

2. How did the pip in sap taste? *(Literal)*

3. How did the wax help Vig get the pip out of the gap? *(Inferential)*

EXTENDING VOCABULARY

gap	What is a *gap?* What is another word that has a similar meaning? If you take away the *g* and put another letter at the start, what new words can you make?
zigs and **zags**	What do these words mean? What is a *zig zag?* Which sound is different in these two words?
zips	How did Vim move in the sentence *She zips to the ant hub?* Did she move slowly or quickly? What other words do you know that have a similar meaning to *zips?*

MOVING BEYOND THE TEXT

1. What do ants eat?

2. What do you know about how ants live?

3. What is sap? Where does it come from?

4. What type of wax is Vig using to get the pip out of the gap?

SPEED SOUNDS

Xx	Yy	Zz		
Kk	Ll	Vv	Qq	Ww
Dd	Jj	Oo	Gg	Uu
Cc	Bb	Rr	Ee	Ff	Hh	Nn
Mm	Ss	Aa	Pp	Ii	Tt

PRACTICE WORDS

zips

Vim

yum

Vig

mix

zigs

wax

zags

fix

Yum

Mix